Arctic Foxes

By Patricia Janes

Children's Press®
An Imprint of Scholastic Inc.

Content Consultant
Nikki Smith
Assistant Curator, North America and Polar Frontier
Columbus Zoo and Aquarium

Library of Congress Cataloging-in-Publication Data
Names: Janes, Patricia, author.
Title: Arctic foxes/by Patricia Janes.
Description: New York, NY: Children's Press, an imprint of Scholastic Inc., [2019] | Series: Nature's children | Includes index.
Identifiers: LCCN 2018023393| ISBN 9780531127131 (library binding) | ISBN 9780531134252 (paperback)
Subjects: LCSH: Arctic fox—Juvenile literature.
Classification: LCC QL737.C22 J36 2019 | DDC 599.776/4—dc23

Design by Anna Tunick Tabachnik

Creative Direction: Judith E. Christ for Scholastic Inc.

Produced by Spooky Cheetah Press

No part of this publication may be reproduced in whole or in part, or stored in a retrieval system,
or transmitted in any form or by any means, electronic, mechanical, photocopying, recording, or otherwise,
without written permission of the publisher. For information regarding permission, write to Scholastic Inc.,
Attention: Permissions Department, Scholastic Inc., 557 Broadway, New York, NY 10012.
© 2019 Scholastic Inc.

All rights reserved. Published in 2019 by Children's Press, an imprint of Scholastic Inc.

Printed in Heshan, China 62

SCHOLASTIC, CHILDREN'S PRESS, NATURE'S CHILDREN™, and associated logos
are trademarks and/or registered trademarks of Scholastic Inc.

6 7 8 9 10 R 28 27 26 25 24 23

Scholastic Inc., 557 Broadway, New York, NY 10012.

Photos ©: cover: Tom Murphy/Getty Images; 1: Mark Sisson/FLPA/Superstock, Inc.; 4 leaf silo and throughout:
stockgraphicdesigns.com; 4 top: Jim McMahon/Mapman ®; 5 fox silo: basel101658/Shutterstock; 5 child silo:
all-silhouettes.com; 5 bottom: Roland Seitre/Minden Pictures; 6 fox silo and throughout: Gallinago_media/Shutterstock;
7: Chris Schenk/Buiten-beeld/Minden Pictures; 8: Andy Trowbridge/Nature Picture Library/Offset.com; 11: Jim Cumming/
Shutterstock; 12: Maria Stenzel/Getty Images; 15: Matthias Breiter/Minden Pictures; 16: Sergey Gorshkov/Minden Pictures;
19 top left: Cory Voecks/EyeEm/Getty Images; 19 top right: Randy Wells/Getty Images; 19 bottom right: Jupiterimages/
Getty Images; 19 bottom left: NHPA/Superstock, Inc.; 20: RGB Ventures/SuperStock/Alamy Images; 23: Steve Kazlowski/
DanitaDelimont.com/Newscom; 25: Art Wolfe/Science Source; 26: Daniel J. Cox/Getty Images; 29: Bart Breet/NIS/Minden
Pictures; 30: Sergey Gorshkov/Minden Pictures; 33: Arterra/UIG/Getty Images; 35: Julie Selan; 36: Pat Gaines/Getty Images;
39: The Granger Collection; 40: Tom Vezo/NPL/Minden Pictures; 42 left: Julius Firl/EyeEm/Getty Images; 42 top right:
Jerry Young/Getty Images; 42 bottom right: Nora Carol Photography/Getty Images; 43 left: Joel Sartore/Getty Images;
43 bottom right: Steven Miley/Design Pics/Getty Images; 43 top right: Mark Sisson/FLPA/Superstock, Inc.

◀ **Cover image shows
an arctic fox curled
up in the snow to
stay warm.**

Table of Contents

Fact File 4

CHAPTER 1   **Symbol of the North** 6
       Home, Sweet Home 9
       Built for the Cold 10
       Extreme Survivor 13

CHAPTER 2   **Coat of Many Colors** 14
       To Be a Fox 17
       Born to Roam 18
       On the Prowl 21
       Settling for Scraps 22

CHAPTER 3   **Family Life** 24
       Preparing the Den 27
       A Kit's Early Days 28
       Growing Up Quickly 31
       Preparing to Go 32

CHAPTER 4   **Clues to the Past** 34
       Close Cousins 37

CHAPTER 5   **A Shared History** 38
       Caution: Melting Snow! 41

Arctic Fox Family Tree 42
Words to Know 44
Find Out More 46
Facts for Now 46
Index 47
About the Author 48

Fact File: Arctic Foxes

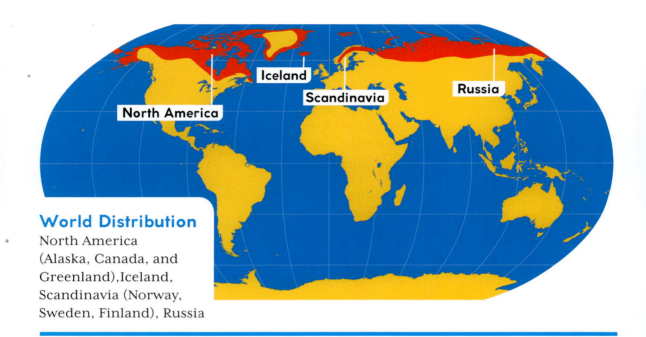

World Distribution
North America (Alaska, Canada, and Greenland), Iceland, Scandinavia (Norway, Sweden, Finland), Russia

Habitat
Arctic and alpine tundra

Habits
Both male and female care for young; live in underground burrows; bury food to survive in harsh winters; may scavenge for food

Diet
Lemmings, voles, birds, eggs, hares, fish, berries, insects, and seaweed

Distinctive Features
Fur coat of different color and thickness depending on the season; long tail used for warmth and balance

Fast Fact
Arctic foxes live farther north than any other fox species.

Average Size

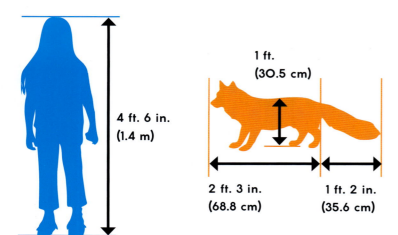

Human (age 10) — 4 ft. 6 in. (1.4 m)

Arctic Fox (adult) — 1 ft. (30.5 cm) tall; 2 ft. 3 in. (68.8 cm) and 1 ft. 2 in. (35.6 cm)

Classification

CLASS
Mammalia
(mammals)

ORDER
Carnivora
(foxes, bears, hyenas, seals, and related animals)

FAMILY
Canidae
(foxes, dogs, wolves, coyotes)

GENUS
Vulpes
(true foxes)

SPECIES
Vulpes lagopus
(arctic foxes)

◀ In winter, an arctic fox blends in perfectly with the snowy landscape.

5

CHAPTER 1

Symbol of the North

A howling wind rages. Snow sweeps across a flat, rocky landscape. Temperatures are well below freezing.

An arctic fox stands motionless. It is invisible against its snowy surroundings. The animal is barely bigger than a house cat, but it is hardy. The fox's thick fur whips around as it sets out in search of food. The extreme cold would cause most animals to freeze to death in hours, if not minutes. But the arctic fox seems unfazed.

This small **mammal** is a member of the dog family. The arctic fox is one of the few animals on Earth that can survive in the harsh **Arctic**. Winters there are long and dark. Summers are sunny, but very short. It takes a special animal to call this land of extremes home.

▶ Touches of gray on this fox's white coat mimic its rocky surroundings.

Home, Sweet Home

Arctic foxes live in the **tundra**, an area in the far north of the planet that is cold and gets little rain. These conditions make it nearly impossible for trees to grow. Low-lying mosses and **lichens** grow there instead. They settle on and between rocks. The nooks and crannies protect them from the extreme weather.

Arctic foxes live in various **habitats**. Many reside inland. Others live along rocky coastlines. Some inhabit hard-to-reach Arctic islands.

Just 48 species of land mammals are able to survive part of the year in the harsh climate of the tundra. The arctic fox is one of them. Other examples include arctic wolves, arctic hares, and caribou. But none of these animals ventures as far north as the arctic fox. It is the only land mammal native to Iceland. (That means it made its way there without the help of humans.) About 800 years ago, huge areas of the Arctic seas froze. Scientists think arctic foxes crossed an ice bridge to get to Iceland.

◀ Some arctic foxes live in the alpine tundra of Norway.

Built for the Cold

The temperature in your kitchen freezer is about 10°F (-12°C). Sounds cold, doesn't it? Compared with temperatures in the Arctic, that's downright toasty! Temperatures in the Arctic can be -40°F (-40°C) for weeks. To survive such bitter cold, an arctic fox needs special **adaptations**.

Foxes that live in warmer regions, such as red foxes, have long legs and ears. That would mean certain death in the far north. Arctic foxes have stubby legs and small ears. Less of the animal's body is exposed to the cold, so less body heat is lost. The fox's long, dense fur helps lock in that heat. Even the undersides of the arctic fox's paws have fur for **insulation**.

Arctic foxes also have a long, fluffy tail called a brush. At bedtime, the fox lays its tail on the snow. It settles onto it like a mattress. Then the fox wraps the rest of its tail around its body like a blanket and nestles its nose underneath. Ah . . . cozy!

Fast Fact
Arctic foxes have hollow hairs that trap body heat.

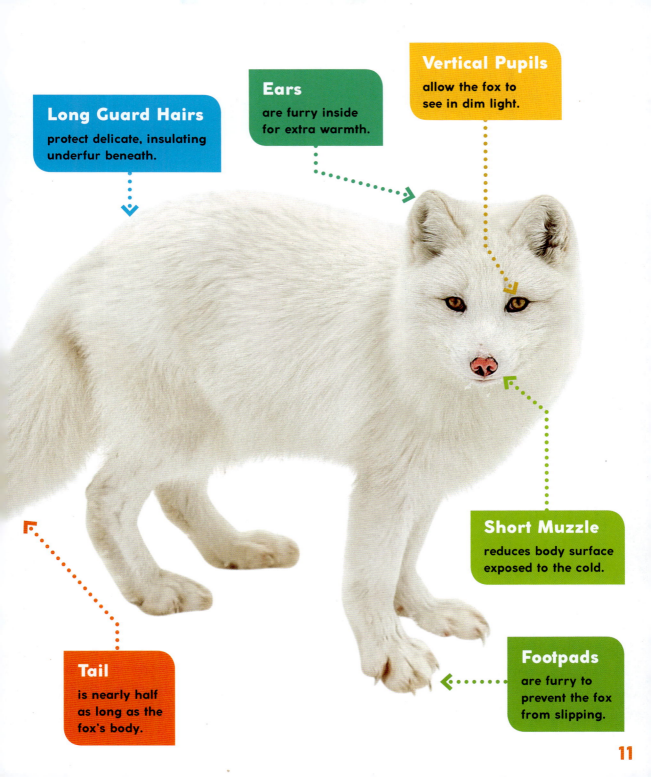

Fast Fact
Arctic foxes have the warmest fur of any animal.

Extreme Survivor

Not all of the arctic fox's amazing adaptations are visible to the naked eye. This winter warrior has a layer of body fat that traps body heat. The arctic fox eats extra food during summer to build up fat. That way it's ready for when temperatures fall.

Arctic foxes also have a special **circulatory system**. Many of their arteries flow next to their veins. Arteries carry warm blood from the heart. Veins carry cooler blood back. Since the two are close together, they can share heat before it has a chance to escape the body.

In winter, food is always scarce in the Arctic. But some winters are especially tough. During these times, an arctic fox can change the rate at which its body uses energy. It can change its body temperature, too. Now the fox's body won't need as much energy to keep warm. That means it won't have to eat as much.

◀ Arctic foxes don't shiver until temperatures drop to around -112°F (-80°C)!

13

CHAPTER 2

Coat of Many Colors

Not all arctic foxes have white fur. It depends on where the fox lives—and the time of year.

Arctic foxes can fall **prey** to polar bears and arctic wolves, so they have to rely on **camouflage** for survival. Having fur that blends in with their surroundings makes it harder for hungry **predators** to spot them.

Arctic foxes living inland have a white coat in winter. It matches the snow on the ground. Between late March and June, the fox begins to **molt**. Clumps of white fur fall out, giving way to dark brown fur. This new coat blends in with the rocks that appear as snow melts.

Arctic foxes living along coasts and on islands have a smoky blue-gray coat all year. It matches the dark rocks along snow-free shorelines.

▶ **This fox has lost most of its winter fur. The animal is almost ready for summer.**

> **Fast Fact**
> Only 21 mammal and bird species change coat colors with the seasons.

To Be a Fox

The arctic fox hasn't only had to adapt physically to its harsh habitat. It has also had to change its behavior.

Most members of the dog family are social. They live together and cooperate. But the arctic fox lives quite a **solitary** life. Arctic foxes come together to **mate** and raise a family. But they spend the cold winter months living alone. That is when food is scarce. It is easier to feed one mouth than many. Because food can be hard to come by, an arctic fox spends most of its active time in search of it.

Arctic foxes are mostly **nocturnal**. They spend the night hours hunting and finding scraps to eat.

◀ An arctic fox chases a snow goose off its nest.

Born to Roam

Arctic foxes are **carnivores**. Their favorite foods include hares and **rodents**, such as lemmings and voles. They dine on fish and bird eggs, too. Still, when times are tough, these meat-eaters will eat almost anything they can find. Sometimes they'll even eat insects, berries, and seaweed.

Some arctic foxes have a small **territory**. Others have a territory that is vast. The size depends on how much food there is. A fox that lives where food is plentiful has it relatively easy. The animal can store food inside the frozen ground for when it isn't readily available. Some arctic foxes live near goose nesting grounds, for example. They may bury up to 3,000 goose eggs to eat later. The home range of these foxes may be only a few square miles.

Other arctic foxes live where food is scarce. They may have to wander hundreds of miles each year. Otherwise they may not find enough food to survive.

▶ An arctic fox's diet varies depending on where it lives and what is available.

Goose Eggs

▶ In places without lemmings, arctic foxes eat bird eggs.

Hare

▶ Arctic foxes will happily dine on arctic hares—if they can catch them!

Lemming

▶ Lemmings are the staple food for arctic foxes in the tundra.

Seaweed

▶ Arctic foxes that live near water eat seaweed, seabirds, and seals.

Fast Fact
The arctic fox is both a predator and a scavenger.

On the Prowl

The arctic fox has a superb sense of smell. This hunter can hear extremely well, too. These traits come in handy when the fox hunts lemmings.

In winter, lemmings live under the snow. The snow guards against cold temperatures and blowing winds. But it can't shield a lemming from a hungry arctic fox. Foxes can smell this tasty treat even when it's hidden under snow as deep as 20 inches (50.8 centimeters).

Once the fox sniffs out its prey, it stops in its tracks. It listens closely. The fox is trying to hear the animal **burrowing** beneath it. Once the fox hears its prey, it positions itself just right. It leaps straight into the air and dives—headfirst—into the snow. Its hind legs and tail wriggle around. The fox looks like it's swimming in snow. With any luck, the fox grabs its victim with its canine teeth. Suppertime!

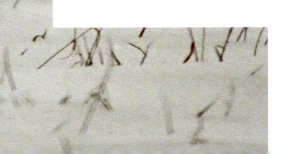

◀ An arctic fox leaps into the air to nab a lemming.

Settling for Scraps

Unfortunately, lemming populations plummet every three to five years. When that happens, arctic foxes have trouble finding enough to eat. As a result, their numbers fall, too. To survive, an arctic fox must **scavenge** for food.

During this time, a fox will often feed on animals that are already dead, such as a whale that has died and washed up on land. The fox may even dine alongside a polar bear in order to pick at a dead animal's remains. This is risky, as polar bears prey on arctic foxes, too.

Polar bears are marine mammals. They live on land and at sea. In winter, sea ice in the Arctic freezes over. Polar bears go onto the ice to hunt for seals and other sea life. The bears eat as much as they want. Then they leave the rest behind for scavengers like foxes.

▶ **Foxes take their lives in their hands when they join in a polar bear's meal.**

CHAPTER 3

Family Life

An arctic fox is ready to mate when it is 10 months old. In February or March, this solitary animal will seek out a mate. It will use its voice to communicate interest in another fox. The call sounds a bit like a cross between a screech and a bark. It may lift its tail or move its ears a certain way, too. If another fox is interested, it will call out in return. The male and female may also chase each other.

Arctic foxes often mate for life. The male and female will go their separate ways for a few months after raising a **litter**. But they will come together the following year to mate again. Arctic foxes usually breed once a year.

▶ **A male and female fox play together in the snow.**

> **Fast Fact**
> A group of foxes is called a skulk or a leash.

Preparing the Den

The female fox will be pregnant for 52 days. After mating, the male and female settle into an underground **den**. This cozy hideaway will protect the couple's babies, called kits, from predators. It will also shelter them from the weather.

Sometimes a pair will dig a new den. But frequently they will use an existing one. Birthing dens are often built into hillsides or riverbanks. An ideal den has good exposure to spring sunlight. It's also high enough that water can't get in.

Most arctic fox pairs—and families—use the same den year after year. Some dens are 300 years old.

Over time the foxes add new tunnels. They add new rooms, too. Dens can get quite large. The biggest on record was the size of a football field. Birthing dens may have as many as 100 exits. But foxes may use only two or three. If there is danger in one part of the den, the fox can escape another way.

◀ As wildflowers replace snow, kits emerge from their dens.

A Kit's Early Days

In May or June, the pregnant female gives birth in the den. There are usually from five to eight kits in a litter. Rarely, litters may have more than 20. Mom and dad will spend the next 100 days raising their young together. Sometimes, a female from a previous litter will help.

A newborn kit weighs just 2 ounces (56.7 grams) at birth. That's about what a tennis ball weighs. The kit is born blind. It won't open its eyes until it is 16 days old. The tiny fox is completely helpless. For the next few months, the den will offer protection from hungry predators such as wolves.

Like other mammals, newborn kits drink milk from their mother. The mother rarely leaves the den in these early days. The female fox relies on her mate to bring food back to the den for her.

▶ A mother fox can nurse many kits at once.

Fast Fact
Most arctic foxes don't survive their first year.

Growing Up Quickly

A kit begins eating meat when it's about one month old. If food is plentiful, one parent will go out to hunt while the other stays in the den to guard the kits. Often, however, both parents must leave to hunt. If food is scarce, that's the only way they can bring back enough food to feed the litter. A kit eats from three to 10 lemmings (or a similar amount of food) each day. A family of foxes can eat up to 18,000 lemmings in three months!

The one-month-old kit will also finally step foot outside the den for the first time. It has just a few more months with its family before it sets out on its own. The kit has a lot to learn before then.

One skill the kit must master is hunting. A juvenile learns by watching its parents catch prey. It also practices by wrestling with siblings. When a young fox is about three months old, it begins to hunt for itself.

◀ A kit practices hunting by tossing around a dead lemming.

31

Preparing to Go

By early fall, the fox family is using its den less often. The juveniles are stronger and more independent now. They no longer need the safety of the den. The family may even leave the den altogether to follow a food source.

When an arctic fox is just 100 days old, it is considered fully grown. By September, the fox will leave its parents. It learned many lessons from them. But there is one skill it will have to figure out all on its own: how to survive an Arctic winter.

The young fox has never experienced the extreme cold of the Arctic. It has never lived through the dark of the northern winter. Nor has it had to find food in the harshest of times. It won't be easy, but with any luck, the fox will live to be about three years old.

▶ **Everything is new to a kit—even other Arctic species like this reindeer.**

CHAPTER 4

Clues to the Past

About 55 million years ago, the first **ancestors** of the modern fox appeared. Animals that share this ancestor are called Carnivora. Over time, this group split into catlike carnivores and doglike carnivores. Foxes, domestic dogs, wolves, and bears are doglike carnivores. These animals hunt prey by outrunning them. Once they catch their prey, they rip it apart. Catlike carnivores stalk their prey. They stab them with their teeth. Even though arctic foxes are members of the dog family, they stalk and pounce on prey the way cats do!

About nine million years ago, the doglike carnivores split into two groups. One group includes large-bodied wolves. The other includes small-bodied foxes. The oldest arctic fox remains ever found belong to an **extinct** species. It is called *Vulpes qiuzhudingi*. It lived 3.6 million to 5 million years ago.

▶ This illustration shows what *Vulpes qiuzhudingi* might have looked like.

Fast Fact
There are 12 species of true foxes.

Close Cousins

Today, foxes are found everywhere except Antarctica. Some live near cities. Others live in the countryside. Some are found in dry deserts. Others prefer cool, wet places. Regardless of these differences, all foxes have certain things in common. They all have long, bushy tails. They all have long, thin pupils in their eyes—like cats. And they all have excellent hearing and vision.

The arctic fox's closest living cousins are the kit fox and the swift fox. The swift fox lives in the grasslands of the western United States and Canada. This small tan fox certainly lives up to its name. The swift fox can run nearly 40 miles (64.4 kilometers) per hour.

The kit fox is the smallest species of the dog family—but it has really big ears! The kit fox lives in the deserts of the United States and Mexico. Heat is released from the fox's ears, helping this desert dweller stay cool.

◀ The swift fox was once in danger of dying out.

CHAPTER 5

A Shared History

Humans have a long history of hunting arctic foxes. The bones of arctic foxes have been found at an ancient hunting camp in Europe. The campsite is 26,000 years old. And 1,000-year-old stone fox traps have been found in some parts of Greenland.

People have hunted arctic foxes more recently, too. In the early 1900s it became fashionable in Europe to wear their fur. Women wore scarves and collars made of arctic fox **pelts**. Often, people native to the north, like the Inuit of Canada, Alaska, and Greenland, would trap the foxes. Then they traded the pelts for goods and money.

During the height of the fur trade, people almost hunted some arctic fox **populations** to extinction. But the species as a whole held on.

▶ **People used to exchange pelts for money and supplies.**

38

Caution: Melting Snow!

Several hundred thousand arctic foxes live in the wild. Overall the species is doing well, but experts fear there may be trouble ahead. Earth's atmosphere is warming. This **climate change** is causing snow and ice to melt.

Lemmings rely on snow. It provides them with warmth. It also protects the plants they eat. Lemmings may not survive if snow melts. With fewer lemmings to eat, arctic foxes could starve. Similarly, polar bears hunt for seals on sea ice. With less ice, polar bears may starve and disappear. Arctic foxes wouldn't be able to depend on polar bears' leftovers.

As Earth warms, the tundra may turn into forest. The arctic fox's white coat would no longer serve as camouflage. It would stand out in a brown and green forest.

Scientists hope people will work to slow climate change. You can do your part by planting a tree or using less electricity. These actions reduce the amount of heat-trapping gases in the atmosphere. With any luck, arctic foxes will continue to roam the north for years to come.

◀ **An arctic fox without camouflage is easily spotted.**

Arctic Fox Family Tree

Arctic foxes belong to the genus *Vulpes*, also known as true foxes. All the animals in this genus are doglike carnivores. This diagram shows how arctic foxes are related to other doglike carnivores and other true foxes, such as kit foxes and red foxes. The closer together two animals are on the tree, the more similar they are.

Gray Wolves
largest wild members of the Canidae family

Fennec Foxes
smallest fox species; enormous ears help release body heat

Dogs
domestic members of the Canidae family

Ancestor of all Doglike Carnivores

42   *Note: Animal photos are not to scale.*

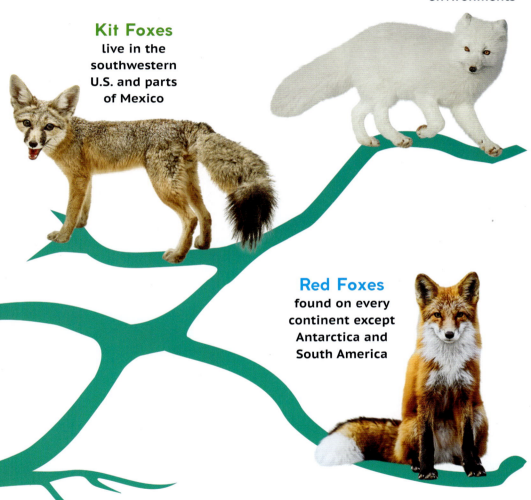

43

Words to Know

A .... **adaptations** *(ad-ap-TAY-shuns)* changes a living thing goes through so it fits in better within its environment

ancestors *(ANN-sess-turs)* family members who lived long ago

Arctic *(AHRK-tik)* the area around the North Pole

B .... **burrowing** *(BUR-oh-ing)* tunneling or digging holes in the ground

C .... **camouflage** *(KAM-uh-flahzh)* a disguise or a natural coloring that allows animals, people, or objects to hide by making them look like their surroundings

carnivores *(KAHR-nuh-vorz)* animals that eat meat

circulatory system *(SER-kyoo-luh-tor-ee SIH-stem)* the group of organs that cause blood to flow through the body

climate change *(KLYE-mat chaynj)* global warming and other changes in weather and weather patterns that are happening because of human activity

D .... **den** *(DEN)* the home of a wild animal

E .... **extinct** *(ik-STINGKT)* no longer found alive

H .... **habitats** *(HAB-i-tats)* the places where an animal or plant is usually found

I .... **insulation** *(IN-suh-lay-shun)* prevention of heat escape

L .... **lichens** *(LYE-kuhnz)* flat, spongelike growths on rocks, walls, and trees that consist of algae and fungi growing close together

litter *(LIH-tur)* a number of baby animals that are born at the same time to the same mother

M .... **mammal** *(MAM-uhl)* a warm-blooded animal that has hair or fur and usually gives birth to live babies; female mammals produce milk to feed their young

mate *(MATE)* to come together to produce offspring

molt *(MOHLT)* to lose old fur, feathers, shell, or skin so that new ones can grow

N .... **nocturnal** *(nahk-TUR-nuhl)* active at night

P .... **pelts** *(PELTZ)* animal skins with the hair or fur still on them

populations *(pahp-yuh-LAY-shuhnz)* all members of a species living in a certain place

predators *(PRED-uh-tuhrs)* animals that live by hunting other animals for food

prey *(PRAY)* an animal that is hunted by another animal for food

R .... **rodents** *(ROH-duhntz)* mammals such as rats, beavers, and squirrels that have large, sharp front teeth that are constantly growing and used for gnawing things

S .... **scavenge** *(SKAV-uhnj)* to search for and collect useful or edible things in waste left behind by another

solitary *(SAH-li-ter-ee)* not requiring or without the companionship of others

T .... **territory** *(TER-i-tor-ee)* an area that an animal or group of animals uses and defends

tundra *(TUHN-druh)* a very cold area of northern Europe, Asia, and North America where there are no trees and the soil under the surface of the ground is always frozen

Find Out More

BOOKS

- Benoit, Peter. *Tundra* (A True Book). New York: Scholastic Inc., 2011.
- Spelman, Lucy. *Animal Encyclopedia*. Washington, D.C.: National Geographic, 2012.
- Taylor, Barbara. *Arctic and Antarctic* (DK Eyewitness Books). Rev. ed. New York: DK Publishing, 2012.

WEB PAGES

- **www.worldwildlife.org/species/arctic-fox**

  Read about the arctic fox and some of the threats these animals face.

- **defenders.org/arctic-fox/basic-facts**

  Learn more about the diet and behavior of arctic foxes, as well as what you can do to protect the species.

- **www.marylandzoo.org/animal/arctic-fox**

  The Maryland Zoo in Baltimore gives basic information about the animals on exhibit—including arctic foxes.

Facts for Now

Visit this Scholastic Web site for more information on arctic foxes:
www.factsfornow.scholastic.com Enter the keywords **Arctic Foxes**

Index

A

adaptations................... 10-11, *11*, 13

ancestors 34

B

birthing....................................... 28

burrowing 21

C

camouflage *5*, *7*, *14*, 17, *40*

carnivores....................................18

circulatory system..........................13

climate change.............................41

communication 24

D

dens *26*, 27

diet................*16*, 17, 18, 19, 20, 21, 22, 23, 28, 31, 41

E

energy conservation.................. *12*, 13

extinction..............................34, 38

F

fur.......................................10, 14, *15*

fur trade 38, *39*

H

habitats 4, 6, *7*, *8*, 9, 10

hunting *16*, 17, *20*, 21, *30*, 31, 34

I

insulation 10

J

juveniles 31, 32

K

kit foxes......................................37

kits *26*, 27, *28*, 29, *30*, 31, 32, 33

L

lemmings................. 18, *19*, 20, 21, 22, *30*, 31, 41

lichens... 9

life expectancy............................ 32

litters 24, 28, 31

M

mammals............................ 9, 17, 22

mating.................................17, *24*, 25

molting......................................14, 15

N

nursing....................................28, 29

P

pelts 38, *39*

polar bears 14, *22*, 23, 41

Index (continued)

P (continued)
predators 14, *22*, 28, 38
prey 18, *19*, 20, 21, 22, 30, 31, 34, 41

R
reindeer *33*
relatives 37
rodents 18

S
scavenging 22, *23*, 41
senses 21, 37
swift foxes *36*, 37

T
territory 18
threats 14, 28, 38, *39*
tundra 8, 9, 41

V
Vulpis qiuzhudingi 34, *35*

About the Author

Patricia Janes has nearly two decades of experience writing about science for children. She once traveled to Churchill, Canada, and saw polar bears and arctic foxes in the wild. She lives with her husband, son, and dog in Westchester, New York—which is very, very far from the frozen north.